WEIRD AND UNUSUAL ANIMALS

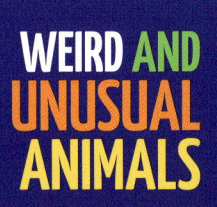

STAR-NOSED MOLES

by Wendy Perkins

AMICUS HIGH INTEREST • AMICUS INK

Amicus High Interest and
Amicus Ink are imprints of Amicus
P.O. Box 1329, Mankato, MN 56002
www.amicuspublishing.us

Copyright © 2018 Amicus. International copyright reserved in all countries. No part of this book may be reproduced in any form without written permission from the publisher.

Library of Congress Cataloging-in-Publication Data
Names: Perkins, Wendy, 1957- author.
Title: Star-nosed moles / by Wendy Perkins.
Description: Mankato, Minnesota : Amicus High Interest, [2018] | Series Weird and unusual animals | Audience: K to grade 3. | Includes bibliographical references and index.
Identifiers: LCCN 2016038825 (print) | LCCN 2016051591 (ebook) | ISBN 9781681511610 (library binding) | ISBN 9781681521923 (pbk.) | ISBN 9781681512518 (ebook)
Subjects: LCSH: Star-nosed mole--Juvenile literature.
Classification: LCC QL737.S76 P47 2018 (print) | LCC QL737.S76 (ebook) | DDC 599.33/5--dc23
LC record available at https://lccn.loc.gov/2016038825

Photo Credits: tets/Shutterstock background pattern; Ken Catania/Visuals Unlimited, Inc. cover; blickwinkel/Alamy Stock Photo 4–5; Dwight Kuhn 2, 7, 10–11, 12–13, 18–19, 20, 22; Ken Catania/Visuals Unlimited, Inc. 8–9; myrrha 15; Skip Moody / Science Source 16–17

Editor: Wendy Dieker
Designer: Aubrey Harper
Photo Researcher: Holly Young

Printed in the United States of America

HC 10 9 8 7 6 5 4 3 2 1
PB 10 9 8 7 6 5 4 3 2 1

TABLE OF CONTENTS

A Strange Star	**5**
Underground Hunters	**6**
Touchy Tools	**9**
Speed Eater	**10**
Pack a Snack	**13**
Little Stars	**14**
Dig In!	**17**
Time to Swim	**18**
Smelling Bubbles	**21**
A Look at Star-Nosed Moles	*22*
Words to Know	*23*
Learn More	*24*
Index	*24*

4

A STRANGE STAR

Here is a star you will not find in the sky. This mole has one on its face! The **feelers** around its nose look like a star's **rays**. That is why it is called a star-nosed mole.

UNDERGROUND HUNTERS

Star-nosed moles live underground. Their fleshy feelers help them find their way in the dark. The feelers find worms and insects to eat. Yum!

Weird but True
Many animals that live in darkness have tiny eyes. Star-nosed moles are no different. They can't see well at all.

7

8

TOUCHY TOOLS

The feelers are called rays. They feel things, just like your fingers do. Tiny bumps cover each ray. These bumps send touch signals to the mole's brain. Is this food? Or grass?

SPEED EATER

These moles are known as the fastest feeders. They feel around. They grab a worm. They eat it down. They do it all faster than you can blink. Gulp!

11

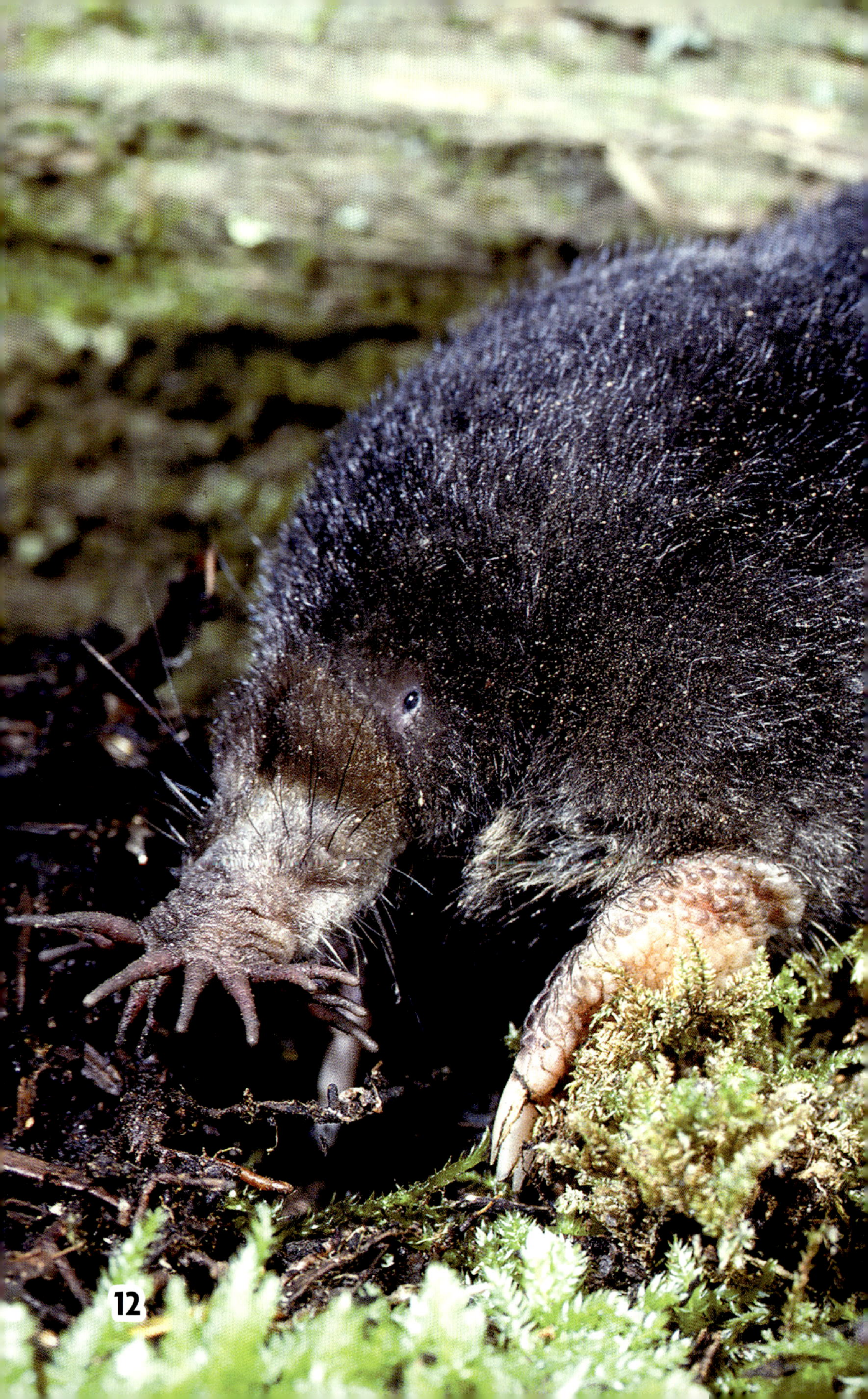

PACK A SNACK

A star-nosed mole's tail grows fat in the fall. In the winter, the mole may not find much food. It uses the fat in its tail to survive. By late spring, the tail is thin again.

LITTLE STARS

Star-nosed moles are small animals. One is about the size of an adult's hand. At birth, they are only about the size of your thumb. The babies grow fast. They can take care of themselves after a month.

15

16

DIG IN!

The star-nosed mole has long claws. They are good for digging. A mole digs **tunnels** just under the surface of the earth. It spends most of its life in its tunnels.

Weird but True
A star-nosed mole can make a tunnel the length of a couch in about one hour. Wow!

TIME TO SWIM

Star-nosed moles live in eastern North America. They live close to water. They dig through wet mud. Many of their tunnels lead to water. Star-nosed moles are good swimmers. They sometimes catch and eat fish.

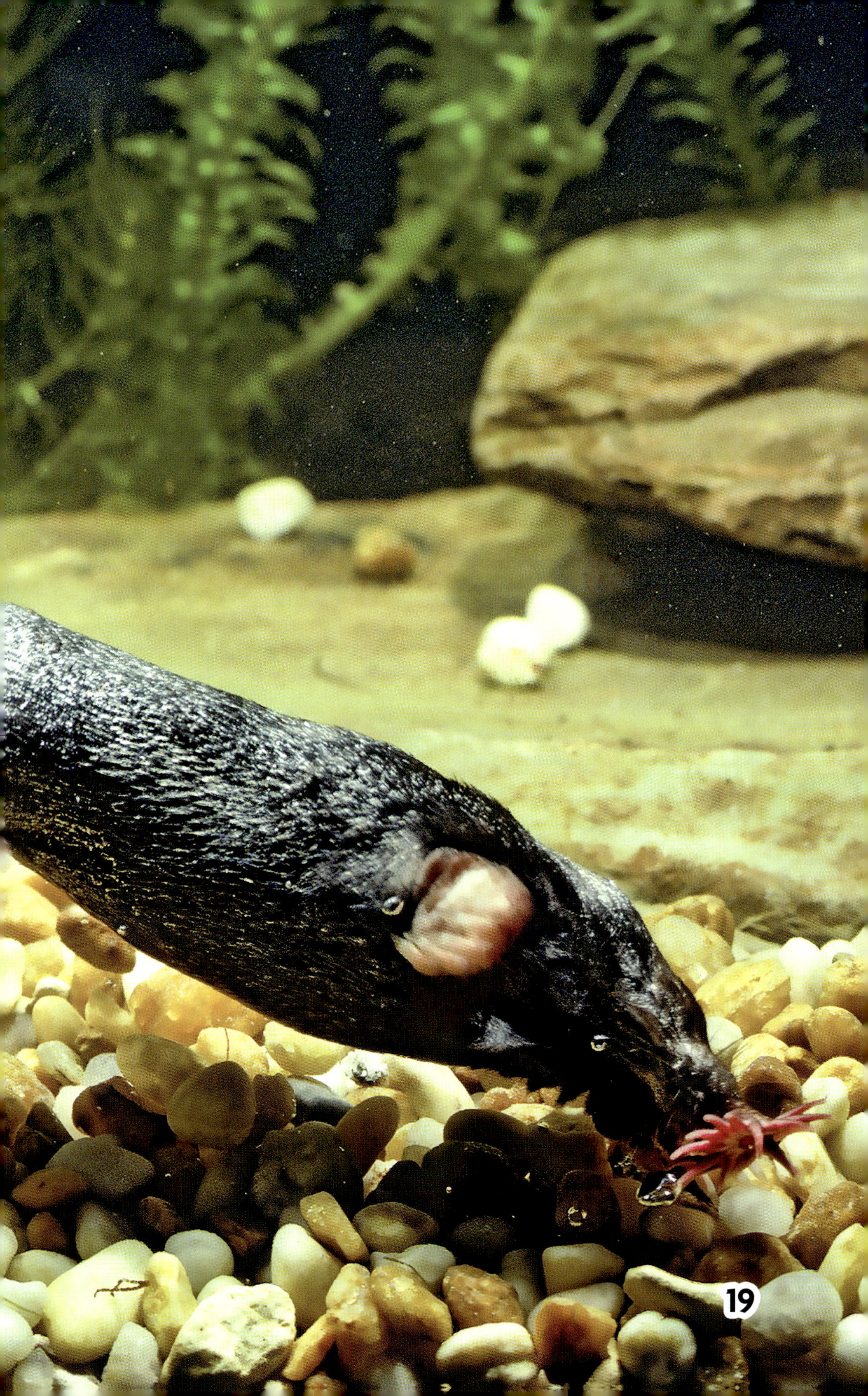

20

SMELLING BUBBLES

Star-nosed moles can even smell underwater. They blow bubbles from their nose. They sniff them back in. The bubbles carry smells from the water. No other **mammal** can do this. This mole's nose is special in many ways!

A LOOK AT STAR-NOSED MOLES

fur

eye

feelers

nostril

claws

22

WORDS TO KNOW

feelers – body parts that are used to touch and get information about what is around

mammal – an animal that has a backbone, is covered in hair, and feeds milk to its babies

ray – a body part that extends out from a center point

tunnel – a long hole underground used to get from one place to another

LEARN MORE

Books
Owings, Lisa. *Star-Nosed Mole*. Pilot. Extremely Weird Animals. Minneapolis: Bellwether Media, 2014.

Zappa, Marcia. *Star-Nosed Moles*. World's Weirdest Animals. Minneapolis: ABDO Publishing, 2016.

Websites
The Beauty of Ugly: Star-Nosed Moles – Nature
www.pbs.org/wnet/nature/the-beauty-of-ugly-star-nosed-moles/428

Easy Science for Kids – All About Moles
http://easyscienceforkids.com/all-about-moles

INDEX

babies 14

claws 17

eating 6, 9, 10, 13, 18

feelers 5, 6, 9

habitat 6, 18

nose 5, 21

size 14

swimming 18, 21

tail 13

tunnels 17, 18

Every effort has been made to ensure that these websites are appropriate for children. However, because of the nature of the Internet, it is impossible to guarantee that these sites will remain active indefinitely or that their contents will not be altered.